That Was Then, This Is Now

S. E. Hinton

TEACHER GUIDE

NOTE:

The trade book edition of the novel used to prepare this guide is found in the Novel Units catalog and on the Novel Units website. Using other editions may have varied page references.

Please note: We have assigned Interest Levels based on our knowledge of the themes and ideas of the books included in the Novel Units sets, however, please assess the appropriateness of this novel or trade book for the age level and maturity of your students prior to reading with them. You know your students best!

BN 978-1-56137-522-6

To order, contact your
local school supply store, or:

Toll-Free Fax: 877.716.7272
Phone: 888.650.4224
3901 Union Blvd., Suite 155
St. Louis, MO 63115

sales@novelunits.com

novelunits.com

Table of Contents

Novel Units: Rationale

How do you ensure that the needs of individual students are met in a heterogeneous classroom? How do you challenge students of all abilities without losing some to confusion and others to boredom?

With the push toward "untracking" our schools, there are questions that more and more educators need to examine. As any teacher of "gifted" or "remedial" students can attest, even "homogeneous" classrooms contain students with a range of abilities and interests. Here are some of the strategies research suggests:

- cooperative learning
- differentiated assignments
- questioning strategies that tap several levels of thinking
- flexible grouping within the class
- cross-curriculum integration
- process writing
- portfolio evaluation

Novel Units Teacher's Guides and *Student Packets* are designed with these seven facets in mind. Discussion questions, projects, and activities are framed to span all of the levels of Bloom's Taxonomy. Graphic organizers are provided to enhance critical thinking and comprehension. Tests and quizzes (included in the Student Packets) have been developed at two levels of difficulty (Level 1=lower; Level 2=higher). While most of the activities in the Teacher's Guides and Student Packets could be completed individually, many are ideal vehicles for collaborative effort.

Throughout the guides, there is an emphasis on collaboration: students helping other students to generate ideas, students working together to actualize those ideas, and students sharing their products with other students. Extension activities link literature with other areas of the curriculum—including writing, art, music, science, history, geography, and current events—and provide a basis for portfolio evaluation.

Finally, teachers are encouraged to adapt the guides to meet the needs of individual classes and students. The open-ended nature of many of the activities makes them useful for most any level.

You know your students best; we are offering you some tools for working with them. On the following page are some of the "nuts and bolts" for using these "tools": a glossary of some of the terms used above that will facilitate your use of the guides.

Bloom's Taxonomy...
is a classification system for various levels of thinking. Questions keyed to these levels may be:
- comprehension questions, which ask one to state the meaning of what is written,
- application questions, which ask one to extend one's understanding to a new situation,
- analysis questions, which ask one to think about relationships between ideas such as cause/effect,
- evaluation questions, which ask one to judge the accuracy of ideas,
- synthesis questions, which ask one to develop a product by integrating the ideas in the text with ideas of one's own.

Graphic Organizers...
are visual representations of how ideas are related to each other. These "pictures"—including Venn diagrams, flow charts, attribute webs, etc.—help students collect information, make interpretations, solve problems, devise plans, and become aware of how they think.

Cooperative Learning...
refers to learning activities in which groups of two or more students collaborate. There is compelling research evidence that integration of social activities into the learning process—such as small group discussion, group editing, group art projects—often leads to richer, more long-lasting learning.

Evaluation Portfolios...
are, literally, portable cases for carrying loose papers and prints. More and more teachers at all levels are utilizing portfolios—product folders—in assessment of student learning.

Process Writing...
is a way of teaching writing in which the emphasis is no longer on the product alone. Rather, students work continuously through the steps of prewriting, drafting, and revision — often through collaborative effort—in order to develop a piece for sharing with a real audience.

Plot Summary

The story is narrated by Bryon, a smart, street-wise 16-year-old. Bryon and his best friend Mark (who lives with Bryon and Bryon's mother) drop in at the local pool hall and learn from Charlie, the bartender and owner, that "M & M"—a bright, friendly young boy who seems to live on M & Ms—is looking for them. When they find M & M at the drugstore reading magazines, he reveals that his older sister Cathy is home after a year spent away. The three boys go to a bowling alley, but M & M—who babysits frequently for his many younger siblings—soon announces that he has to leave. Shortly after he leaves, he is attacked by Curly Shepard and two other teens, who cut off his peace medallion before they are fought off by Mark and Bryon.

The next afternoon, while visiting his mother in the hospital, Bryon meets M & M's sister Cathy, who works in the hospital snack bar. Bryon and Mark visit another patient, Mike Chambers, who has been badly beaten. Mike, who is white, explains that he got beaten up by a group of African Americans while taking a young African woman home (to help her escape racial harassment by a group of young white men at the bus stop).

Bryon, who recently broke up with Angela (who dumped him while making an unsuccessful play for Ponyboy Curtis), arranges to go out with Cathy and gets Charlie to lend him his car. Wearing a beautiful shirt that Mark happened to "find" on the street, Bryon meets Cathy's family and takes her to a dance. Mark goes to the dance "stag" with Ponyboy Curtis, and both are attacked by Angela's brothers. Ten stitches later, Mark is released by the hospital and while he rests, the two spend the next afternoon reminiscing about the "good times" they've had: hot-wiring cars, drunken poker games, pool hustling. While Mark waxes nostalgic about the old gang, Bryon points out that it's good to know your own personality; "that was then and this is now."

Mark gets caught using the principal's car to visit his parole officer, but is able to charm the principal with his personality and stays out of trouble. Later he and Bryon decide to make money by pool hustling at Charlie's. After making a bundle from a couple of Texans, the boys are jumped by them outside. To Bryon's horror, when Charlie comes to their aid, he is shot and killed. As Bryon gets closer to Cathy, the enmity between Cathy and Mark becomes more pronounced.

After M & M runs away from home, Bryon and Cathy look for him for weeks to no avail. Mark suggests that he and Bryon pick up Angela, who has obviously been drinking; she passes out and Mark cuts off her hair. Later, Tim and Curly Shepard retaliate by beating up Bryon, who asks a tearful Mark not to go after his attackers.

Mark tips off Bryon and Cathy to the fact that M & M has been staying at a "hippie" commune. When Bryon and Cathy locate M & M, he is having a "bad trip;" they take him to the hospital, where a doctor explains that M & M may never be the same again, mentally. Shaken, Bryon returns home and looks under Mark's mattress for a cigarette. There he finds a stash of drugs and realizes that Mark is a pusher. Enraged after seeing what drugs have done to M & M, Bryon calls the police, who take Mark away later that night.

Bryon's feelings for Cathy are shattered; he stops seeing her and she starts going out with Ponyboy Curtis. Mark is sentenced to five years in a reformatory; when Bryon finally is allowed to see Mark, Mark says that he hates Bryon and it is clear that Mark will never forgive him. At the end of the story, Bryon is depressed, apathetic, and confused. "I am too mixed up to really care...I wish I was a kid again, when I had all the answers."

Background on the Novelist

S.E. Hinton was only 16 when she wrote her first novel, *The Outsiders*. Since then, she has written *That Was Then, This is Now; Rumble Fish; Tex;* and *Taming the Star Runner.* She lives with her husband and son in Oklahoma.

Initiating Activities

Choose one or more of the following activities to establish an appropriate mind set for the story students are about to read:

1. **Anticipation Guide** *(See Novel Units Student Packet, Activity #1):* Students discuss their opinions of statements which tap themes they will meet in the story. For example:
   (a) Once you have a girl/boyfriend, your friendship with your best friend is bound to suffer.
   (b) It's okay for teenagers to drink, as long as they don't drive.
   (c) Most parents don't really have any idea what their kids are doing.
2. **Log:** Have students keep a response log as they read.
   (a) In one type of log, the student assumes the persona of one of the characters. Writing on one side of each piece of paper, the student writes in the first person ("I...") about his or her reactions to one episode in that chapter. A partner (or the teacher) responds to these writings on the other side of the paper, as if talking to the character.

		Dual Entry Log	
pp.	*Summary*		*Reactions* (These might begin: I liked the part where...", "This reminded me of the time I...", "This character reminds me of another character..." "If I were this character, I wouldn't..." "I disagree with this character...")

(b) In the dual entry log (above), students jot down brief summaries and reactions to each section of the novel they have read. (The first entry could be made based on a preview of the novel— a glance at the cover and a flip through the book.)

3. **Verbal Scales:** After students finish a section of the story, have them chart their feelings and judgments about various characters using the following scales or others you construct. Students should discuss their ratings, using evidence from the story.

Like	1-2-3-4-5-6	Dislike
Happy	1-2-3-4-5-6	Sad
Active	1-2-3-4-5-6	Passive
Honest	1-2-3-4-5-6	Dishonest
Caring	1-2-3-4-5-6	Unkind
Responsible	1-2-3-4-5-6	Irresponsible
Proud	1-2-3-4-5-6	Modest
Rich	1-2-3-4-5-6	Poor
Sympathetic	1-2-3-4-5-6	Self-absorbed

4. **Brainstorming:** Have students generate associations with a theme that is central to the story while a student scribe jots ideas around the central word or statement on a large piece of paper. Help students "cluster" the ideas into categories. Students might brainstorm about these ideas:

- teen drinking and drug use
- teen relationships with parents
- teen gangs
- teen pranks and actual crimes

- teen friendships
- teen relationships with the opposite sex
- why friends often grow apart

Sample framework for "Growing Apart":

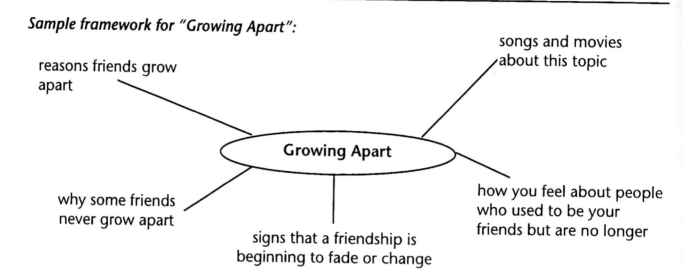

5. **Role Play:** Have small groups of students improvise skits demonstrating one of the following situations (analogous to a situation that is central to the story):
   - You find out that your friend has broken the law.
   - You see someone being bullied.
   - You're in the middle—between two friends of yours who dislike each other.

6. **Discussion or Writing:**
   - **Friendship:** What is friendship, to you? How far should you be willing to go for a friend? Friendship can be abused and used selfishly. Can you think of examples from literature—or from your life?

   - **Drug and Alcohol Use:** Are street drugs worse than alcohol? Should the drinking age be lowered? Why do so many teenagers drink? Is there such a thing as drinking "responsibly" if you are a teenager? What's the problem with drinking—if you don't drive at the same time?

   - **Growing Up:** How are you different from when you were younger? How are you the same? What are some signs of "growing up"? What's good about growing up? What are the disadvantages?

   - **Race Relations during the 1960's/early 1970's:** Who were the Black Panthers? How were African Americans treated in this country during the 1960's? What civil rights did they win? What sorts of discrimination did they encounter? What incidents have you seen in documentaries or read about?

- **Parents:** What do you think are the qualities of a "good parent"? How much should they know about your life? What rules should they have? What freedoms should they allow you?

- **Dissatisfaction with Self:** Do you like who you are? Do you ever do things you regret? Do you ever act in a way that surprises you? How much of your behavior is influenced by what others around you are doing? When are you willing to do something because it is what you think is right for you—even though those around you disagree? In what cases do you think it is best to conform? When is it best to break away from "the crowd"?

7. **Prediction:** Have students predict what the story might be about based on the title and cover illustration. What does the expression, "That was then, this is now" mean? In what tone of voice might you say that? What can you tell about the three people on the cover? About how old are they? What can you tell about them from their clothes? from the expressions on their faces? Why do you think there is a police car in the background? Have you read anything else by S. E. Hinton? What sorts of stories does she write? What do you think the mood of the story will be?

8. View the video *That Was Then, This is Now,* starring Emilio Estevez (rated PG-13). Viewing the video <u>before</u> reading is sometimes motivating for reluctant readers. After reading, the movie and novel can be compared. Call Novel Units to order the film.

Vocabulary, Discussion Questions
Writing Ideas, Activities

Chapters 1-2

Vocabulary

adjoining 1	profound 4	compact 5	hot-wire 8
unaffected 8	limerick 9	disarming 10	objected 12
taunting 12	stranglehold 13	sprawling 14	wistful 14
winced 15	lanky 23	authority 23	staggering 23

Discussion Questions:

1. What is Bryon like? (See the description of an Attribute Web on the next page and begin one.) Is he someone you would have for a friend? (Bryon is dark, large, drinks beer, gets into fights, doesn't like police and other authority figures.)

2. How do Bryon and Mark get along? Why do you think they are such good friends? How are they different? (They are like brothers and have lived under the same roof for years; they are both street-wise and enjoy challenging authority—but only Mark sees nothing wrong with stealing, has a way of "getting away with things.")

3. How does Bryon know Charlie? How does Charlie treat Bryon? Do you think Charlie should allow Bryon and Mark into his pool hall? (Bryon used to date Charlie's sister; Charlie is friendly with Bryon—as a big brother might be—but draws the line when Bryon asks for a drink, for a loan, etc.)

4. Who is M & M? What is your impression of him? (M & M is a bright, gentle, long-haired 13-year-old who likes to read, babysit, wears a peace medallion, eats M&M's.)

5. Who gangs up on M & M? What do you think would have happened if Mark and Bryon hadn't stepped in? Why do you think Mark and Bryon get involved in the fight? (Curly Shepard and two others call M & M "flower child" and jump him.)

6. Why does M & M get angry with Bryon and Mark? Whose idea is it to jump the man standing at the light? (They rescue him from being attacked for being different—a "flower child"—then consider attacking someone else because of racial differences; Mark is the one who suggests jumping the black man.)

7. What is Bryon's attitude toward stealing? What is Mark's attitude? (Mark sees nothing wrong with it, but Bryon feels that theft is wrong and draws the line at hustling.)

8. Who is Randy? Why do you suppose Mark acts interested in Randy's description of the commune, while Bryon finds the whole thing boring? (Randy is a "hippie" who picks up Mark and Bryon as hitchhikers. Like the black man, Randy is "different" and Mark may have preconceived ideas about hippies in general.)

9. Who is Cathy? Where does Bryon bump into her? How has she changed? (Cathy is M & M's sister, home from private school, which she paid for herself; she has a job in the hospital cafeteria; the braces on her teeth are gone, her hair is long, and she is beautiful now.)

10. Why is Mike in the hospital? How does he feel about what happened to him? Do you think that could still happen today? (Mike saw a black girl being harassed by some white boys and offered to drive her home; she accepted, but turned on him when they arrived in her black neighborhood and as a result, he was beaten; Mike isn't angry with his attackers or with the girl.)

Vocabulary Activity: Word mapping is an activity that lends itself to any vocabulary list. For words that have clear antonyms, the following framework is suitable:

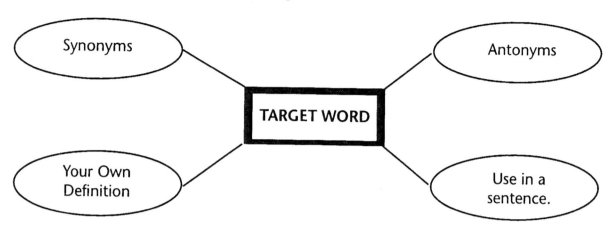

Synonyms

Antonyms

TARGET WORD

Your Own Definition

Use in a sentence.

Variation: Instead of listing antonyms, students can provide line drawings or magazine cut-outs to illustrate the target word, or a mnemonic device (trick for remembering the word's meaning).

Prediction: Will Bryon and Mark see Mike again? Bryon has been trying to get a job. Will he get one? At the end of the chapter, Bryon says that he didn't think much about it—at the time—when Mark said that he'd hate someone for the rest of his life if that person hurt him. Why do you suppose Bryon thinks about it until he thinks he's going crazy now?

Writing Activity: Memory. Bryon has a bad memory of being beaten up by two police officers. He believes that the reason he can't accept authority now is partly because of what happened then. Describe a bad memory you have—and its lasting effect on your behavior or attitudes.

Literary Analysis: Point of view is the position from which a story is told. In the first-person point of view, a character tells the story, using the pronouns "I" and "me". In the third person point-of view, the story-teller is not a character in the story. Elicit from students the fact that this story is told from the first-person point of view. Have students discuss the advantages and disadvantages of this point of view. How would the story be different if it had been told by another character, such as Bryon's mother, or by an all-knowing narrator?

Using Character Attribute Webs—in the Novel Unit Approach

Attribute Webs are simply a visual representation of a character's traits. They provide a systematic way for students to organize and recap the information they have about that particular character. Attribute Webs may be used after reading the story or completed gradually as information unfolds—done individually, or finished as a group project. One type of Character Attribute Web uses these categories:

- How a character acts and feels (What do his or her statements reveal about feelings? What does his or her behavior show you about him or her? In a play—what do the character's gestures, facial expressions, tone of voice tell you about his or her emotions?)
- How a character looks (What do clothing and physique tell you about this character?)
- Where a character lives (In what country, state, neighborhood, does this character live? During what time period?)
- How others feel about the character (What do others' statements and actions show about their attitude toward the character?)

In group discussion about the students' completed Attribute Webs for specific characters, the teacher can ask for supportive evidence from the story. Attribute Webs need not be confined to characters. They can also be used to organize information about a concept, object, or place.

Attribute Webs are a kind of semantic mapping. Students can move on from character webs to other creative kinds of mapping. They can be encouraged to modify Attribute Webs—use subdivisions, add divisions, change connections—in whatever ways are useful to them personally.

Advanced students may be asked to add "spokes" to each trait they identify, citing details or proof from the novel on the added lines. They should be encouraged to write notes in the margins and add thoughts and ideas at random. (The best maps aren't usually the prettiest and neatest!)

It is important to emphasize that Attribute Webs are just a graphic way to record ideas. They provide students with a tool for helping them generate ideas and think about relationships among them.

Basic Attribute Web

How Character Acts

1. _____
2. _____
3. _____
4. _____

How Character Feels

1. _____
2. _____
3. _____
4. _____

Character

Where Character Lives

1. _____
2. _____
3. _____
4. _____

How Others Act & Feel

1. _____
2. _____
3. _____
4. _____

Chapters 3-4

Vocabulary

plainclothes 37	illegitimate 57	hub 61	reminiscing 61
rueful 61	sympathized 63	folk-hero 63	liberals 64
integration 64	probation 67		

Discussion Questions:

1. Why does Bryon admire Charlie? Would you? (Charlie is a high school dropout, but now has his own business, reads a lot, and is respected by police and rough guys alike.)

2. Mark knows Bryon very well and sometimes Bryon finds that irritating. Can you think of an incident that demonstrates this? (Mark knows that the reason Bryon doesn't like Curtis is that Angela dumped Bryon in hopes of attracting Curtis.)

3. How does Mark help Bryon get ready for his date? Do you think Bryon should accept the "gift"? (He gives Bryon a nice shirt—probably stolen.)

4. What is Cathy's family like? Would you like to be a member of this family? (There are lots of children; the father criticizes M & M for his hair and for flunking math and gym.)

5. Why does Angela "flounce off" when Bryon mentions Curtis? In what tone of voice do you imagine Bryon saying, "She wasn't famous for an even temper" (p. 49)? (She is miffed that Curtis isn't attracted to her; Bryon uses an ironic tone.)

6. What happens when Angela tries to get revenge on Curtis? Bryon has threatened the boy who beat up Mark. Do you think Bryon will also try to get back at Angela? (She gets someone to attack Curtis, but it is his friend, Mark, who gets badly hurt.)

7. Bryon and Mark start remembering the "old days." Which of these memories can you relate to—if any? (They recall sneaking into the drive-in, getting caught and jumping out of the manager's truck en route to the police, hot-wiring cars, etc.)

8. How have things changed since the days when Bryon and Mark belonged to a gang? How do Bryon and Mark feel differently about these changes? (Mark feels nostalgic for the days of "all for one and one for all;" Bryon is glad that he doesn't need the gang to make decisions for him anymore.)

9. On the Monday after Mark gets beaten up, Bryon is suspicious of the "Socs." Why? Do you think he is right to be suspicious? Does he remain suspicious? (He suspects that the higher-status "Socs" only pretend to be his friends to be liberal; the talk with Mark has made him think about his place in the group, and how he is affected by conformity.)

10. It seems to Bryon that Mark can get away with anything. Provide one example. Have you ever had a friend who could get away with anything? Do you think Bryon is jealous of Mark? (Mark takes the principal's car to visit his parole officer and manages to make the principal laugh when he is caught.)

Prediction: What sorts of trouble will Mark and Bryon run into in future chapters?

Writing Activity: Reminiscence. Bryon and Mark spend the afternoon talking about when they were "little kids." Describe some of the things you and your best friend used to do together when you were little.

Literary Analysis: The theme is the author's message. Sometimes the theme is stated directly and sometimes it is not. What a character learns, the title, and a particular statement by a character are all sometimes clues to theme. Have students locate where the title words appear in the text (p. 62). What does Bryon mean? How do his words reflect the fact that he and Mark are growing apart?

Chapters 5-6

Vocabulary

expelled 69	obligingly 71	sauntered 75	impersonally 82
vengeful 83	celebrities 83	dependent 84	absently 85
incredulous 85	stimulants 86	dryly 90	analyzed 91
hostility 92			

Discussion Questions:

1. What is your impression of Bryon's mother? (She is kind, loves animals, but doesn't pay a lot of attention to where Mark and Bryon are or what they're doing, and doesn't seem to want to know the details when they get into trouble.)

2. Why do Bryon and Mark ask M & M for $5? Do you think they are taking advantage of him? What does his response—giving them the money—show about him? Do you think they will give the money back the next day, as promised? (They plan to do some pool hustling and need money to start with.)

3. Why do the Texans attack Mark and Bryon? Do you think they should have "seen it coming"? (They are angry about being hustled out of a lot of money during the pool game.)

4. How does Charlie get killed? What is the difference in the way Bryon and Mark react to his death? (Charlie tries to defend Bryon and Mark, and gets shot in the head; Bryon feels guilty, while Mark takes the attitude that "Things happen...")

5. How does Cathy feel about Bryon's admission that he has smoked marijuana? Do you think she feels the same way about his drinking beer? Why or why not? (She doesn't like the idea of his smoking dope and asks him to stop, perhaps because it is a more serious offense than underage drinking.)

6. Why does Mark punch a passenger riding in the Corvette? What do you think he should have done? How does Cathy feel about it? (The passenger made an obscene comment; Cathy thinks Mark is being macho and doesn't approve of his hitting the guy.)

7. According to Bryon, why do kids spend so much time driving up and down "the Ribbon"? Is he blaming adults? Do you think they are to blame? (Bryon points out that adults don't give the young people alternative activities.)

8. Why does M & M get out of the car? What do you think his sister should have done? (He is looking for some friends, running away from home.)

Prediction: Where do you think M & M has gone? What will happen to him?

Writing Activity: Letter. Pretend you are Bryon. After Charlie dies, you decide to write to his sister—the girl you used to date. Tell her what happened and how you feel about it.

Chapters 7-8

Vocabulary

irrationally 98   gulf 101   witticism 121

Discussion Questions:

1. How do Cathy's parents take the news that M & M has run away? Is that how your parents would react? Are they to blame? (The parents and children are upset, but the father says that M & M is going through a "stage" and will return the next day.)

2. Mark is bringing home a lot of money. Where does Bryon think he is getting it? Do you think Bryon is right? Where else could the money be coming from? (Bryon thinks that Mark is winning the money in poker games.)

3. Why does Mark invite Angela for a ride? How does she get drunk? Why is she unhappy? (He is angry that she was responsible for the attack on Curtis and him and wants revenge; she is unhappy with her new marriage.)

4. What does Mark do with the scissors? How do you react to what he does? How does Bryon react? Why doesn't he stop Mark? How do you think Angela will react? (He cuts off Angela's hair; Bryon is too drunk to think about what's happening.)

5. What kind of job does Bryon have? Do you think he'll keep it? (He packs groceries.)

6. Who beats up Bryon? What do you think would have happened if Mark had been around? Why won't Bryon let Mark go after them? What does this show you about how Bryon has changed? (Angela's brothers attack Bryon; Bryon wants to stop the cycle of attacks and counterattacks.)

Prediction: Bryon and Cathy are going steady. How long do you think this will last?

Writing Activity: Reflection. Pretend you are Bryon, resting in bed after the Shepards attacked you. You reflect on your life and how you've been going in circles; you start to think about what your life will be like ten years from now. Write down two versions of your future— a) if you continue as you are, and b) if you "get it together." Then make a list of the things you can do right away to change your life for the better. (You can try this same exercise with your "real self" as the subject.)

Chapters 9-10

Vocabulary

relapse 125	commune 127	barren 128	glorify 129
contorted 132	cylinder 139	throwback 142	

Discussion Questions:

1. Where do Bryon and Cathy find M & M? How do they handle his problem? What else could they have done? Do you think they will tell the police about the "hippies" who are taking drugs? Should they? (Mark tells Bryon where he has seen M & M; M & M is having a bad trip after taking LSD at a "hippie" commune; they drive M & M to the hospital, where his father is waiting.)

2. Why does Bryon get angry with the doctor? Have you ever gotten angry with someone who is the "bearer of bad news"? What expression does this bring to mind? (He doesn't want to hear the doctor's guarded prognosis—that Bryon's mind may never be the same; "Don't kill the messenger.")

3. How does Bryon discover that Mark has been selling drugs? Do you think he suspected before? (Upset after taking M & M to the hospital, Bryon looks for cigarettes under Mark's mattress and finds drugs.)

4. Why does Bryon turn Mark in? Would it make any difference if he knew that Mark hadn't sold the drugs that M & M took? Was turning Mark in the right thing to do? Would he have done it if M & M hadn't just had a bad trip? (Bryon is horrified by the thought that Mark is involved in dealing drugs like the ones that have made M & M so sick and have devastated Cathy's family. His call to the police seems to be an instinctive reaction—we see the "good" in Bryon triumph over the "bad"—and the line is now clearly drawn between Mark and Bryon.)

Prediction: Do you think Bryon will regret turning Mark in? What will Bryon's mother say about it?

Writing Activity: Dream. Put yourself in Bryon's place. It takes a long time to get to sleep after the police come for Mark, but finally you drift off and begin to dream. Describe your dream. Include visual images and other sensory impressions.

Board Activity: Explain the following hypothetical situation to students:

You and your best friend are walking to school. A car pulls up next to you at the curb. In it are two unfamiliar young men a little older than you and your friend. Your friend starts over to the car, but when you follow, waves you back and calls "You go ahead—I'll see you at school." You walk ahead, but glance back over your shoulder and see some kind of exchange going on. You're pretty sure your friend is selling drugs to the two people in the car. Several years ago, the two of you swore to each other that you would never to get involved in drugs.

Now have the students brainstorm solutions. What possible actions might be taken? List these on the chalkboard.

Next, have the students identify criteria for decision-making, such as "Will this keep my friend out of trouble?"..."Will this convince my friend to stop dealing drugs?"..."Will this put me in danger?" Apply the criteria to each possible solution. Try to reach an agreement on the best action to be taken.

You may also want to take time to allow students to relate, in writing or orally, a similar situation they have actually experienced, or one they fear could happen.

Chapter 11

Vocabulary

mechanically 146	impersonally 147	formalities 147	flashback 149
emotional 149	obscure 150	sinister 152	probation 153
parole 153			

Discussion Questions:

1. What sentence does Mark receive? What is his attitude throughout the trial? (He is sentenced to five years in the state reformatory; he acts insolent.)

2. How has M & M changed? (His hair is shorter, he is thin and pale and seems suspicious, worried about flashbacks.)

3. Why does Bryon stop seeing Cathy? Does he blame her for Mark's trouble? How do you suppose she reacts to the way he treats her in the days after M & M's bad trip? (He no longer feels he loves her and is in fact feeling numb to all feelings after turning in his best friend; she is hurt at first, but soon begins seeing Ponyboy Curtis.)

4. Why does it take Bryon so long to go to see Mark? How can you tell that he is trying to "make up" with Mark? Do you think Mark will ever forgive him? Should he? (Mark kept getting into trouble at the reformatory and was denied visitors for a while; Bryon talks about getting Mark a job at the store; Mark says that he hates Bryon.)

Writing Activity: Dialogue. Imagine that Bryon had confronted Mark instead of calling the police. Write the conversation they have.

Literary Analysis: A simile is a comparison that usually contains the words "like" or "as." Point out the simile on page 152 ("He seemed to be pacing, like an impatient, dangerous, caged lion.") Have students discuss how Mark is like a lion. Have them look through the book to find other similes, and for other references to Mark's animal-like qualities.

Extend the activity by discussing the expression "animalistic" and "like an animal" to describe someone who is crude, rude, and unfeeling. How accurate is the use of such an expression? What kinds of animals do people have in mind when they use such expressions? In what ways does/doesn't Mark act like the lion to which Bryon compares him?

Post-Reading Extension Activities

Post-Reading Discussion Questions:

1. How did you feel when you finished this story? Did you feel sorry for anyone? If so, why? What parts made you feel happy? angry? frightened?

2. How do you think Bryon's mother felt after the events in the story? Support your views by including information about her found in the novel.

3. How has Bryon changed? Why? Why do you think he broke it off with Cathy?

4. What do you imagine finally happened to M & M? Would he be able to finish school and support himself? What is the worst-case scenario?

5. What do you think will become of Mark?

6. There are a number of crises and/or tragedies in the lives of the characters in the novel—either described or mentioned. List these.

7. Is it realistic that Bryon's mother has so little involvement in the lives of the boys? Do you think she should have realized something was wrong when Mark first got arrested, and taken some kind of action to prevent future problems? What could she have done, if anything? What would your parents do if you were arrested?

8. How satisfying did you find the ending? How else might the novel have ended?

9. What objections do you think some adults might raise to teaching this book in the classroom? How would you respond? For example, how would you answer someone who objects to the use of profanity by Bryon?

10. Does this novel have any heroes? Who? Why?

Suggested Further Reading

Other books on similar themes (gangs, teenage friendship, peer pressure, alienation):

Bennett, James. *I Can Hear the Mourning Dove.*
Cannon, A. E. *The Shadow Brothers.*
Childress, Alice. *A Hero Ain't Nothing but a Meatball Sandwich.*
Cormier, Robert. *The Chocolate War.*
Dines, Carol. *Best Friends Tell the Best Lies.*
Hopper, Nancy J. *The Truth or Dare Trap.*
Maguire, Jesse. *On the Edge.*
Myers, Walter Dean. *The Young Landlords; Scorpions; Hoops.*
Ure, Jean. *The Other Side of the Fence.*
Salinger, J.D. *Catcher in the Rye.*
Shulman, Irving. *West Side Story.* (the play or novelization)

Other Books by S. E. Hinton:
The Outsiders
Rumble Fish
Tex
Taming the Star Runner

Writing

1. Write a character sketch of Charlie. What kind of man is he? What are his goals and ambitions? How does he feel about himself, his work, the young people who come in?

2. Write a description of someone who reminds you of a character in the story (without giving the person's real name).

3. Write a newspaper article or obituary reporting Charlie's death.

4. Write your own short-story version of *That Was Then, This is Now*—using some real life people you are acquainted with (but changing the names).

5. Write a confession poem, with Bryon as the speaker.

6. Write a case-worker's report on Mark—two months after he has been sentenced for selling drugs.

7. Write the letter Bryon's mother might write to the juvenile authorities in charge of the state reformatory where Mark is being held. Include her impressions of Mark—and her ideas on what might help him.

8. Explain what you think S. E. Hinton's message to young people is.

9. Some things in this novel now seem "dated," for instance, the hippie commune, and the language. If the novel was updated, how would it change? Do you think it is still effective in spite of being dated somewhat?

10. Compare the characters of Angela and Cathy. Did either or both of them remind you of people you know? What do you imagine their futures will be like?

11. Write titles for each chapter.

12. Explain exactly why you think Bryon decided to call the police when he found the drugs under Mark's mattress?

13. Make a list of five problems you have faced (such as problems involving friends, parents, not achieving a goal, being frightened about something). Choose one of these problems. Then invent a character and give the problem to him or her. Write a story in which your character deals with the problem.

Listening/Speaking

1. Give an oral report on parts of the story that especially interested you. For example, you might be interested in parts of the story that deal with loyalty between friends. What does the word "loyalty" mean to you? Use various characters and incidents from the story to support your ideas.

2. Form a panel to discuss drug-dealing in your community. Formulate possible solutions.

3. Discuss how young drug-dealers are penalized in your community. Debate whether the penalties are appropriate.

4. Imagine that you are interviewing Bryon for a TV special on drug use among adolescents. Write your interview questions, then tape your "interview" with another student role-playing Bryon.

Drama

1. Form small groups and act out one or two scenes from the story (such as the scene where Mark realizes he needs a ride to get to the meeting with the parole officer and the scene where Bryon talks to Cathy after Mark has been taken away). Show what happened—and then show how the situation could have been handled better.

2. Write and act out a scene that didn't happen in the story—but might have. For example: How would Mark have reacted if he found himself in jail—after an anonymous tip alerted police to his drug-dealing? When Bryon and Mark were the best of friends, how do you suppose they might have celebrated Bryon's birthday? After Bryon turned Mark in, the next two months were a "blur." Suppose Bryon had had a meeting with his guidance counselor to talk about how things were going. What do you suppose each might have said?

3. Stage Mark's trial.

Viewing

1. Watch the film *That Was Then, This is Now.*

   Before viewing: Discuss and list in small group how you picture the actors in key roles will look. List the most important scenes in the novel. With which scene would you open the film? With which would you close it? What kind of music would you include?

   During viewing: Take notes regarding actors, music, and scenes included.

   After viewing: Compare your pre-viewing lists with the notes you took during the movie. How did the film differ from the book? Which did you like better?

Follow-up: With a partner, write a review of the film for the movie section of your newspaper and a review of the novel for the book section.

Art

1. Draw a picture illustrating any incident in the book which interests you.

2. Form a group and draw a mural depicting some of the major scenes from the book.

3. Graffiti Wall. Discuss what graffiti is, why people write it, what some examples are. Have students create a city skyline by cutting or drawing the outlines of tall buildings on a long roll of butcher paper. Fasten the skyline to a bulletin board or wall. Beneath it, place a blank piece of butcher paper representing a wall. After students complete each two-chapter section of the book, have them "step into a character's shoes" and write graffiti messages on the wall. The messages should express the character's feelings about him/herself or about someone or something else. Messages should be written from left to right so that they are found on the wall in the order in which related events happen in the book.

4. Make a mobile by cutting a paper plate in half and punching five or six holes along the straight edge. Attach strings. From these, suspend pictures of items that have significance in the story (e.g., M & M's peace symbol, Bryon's cue stick, Mark's pack of cigarettes, Angela's cut-off hair). On the back of each, write a short explanation of the part the item plays in the story.

Music

1. Choose appropriate background music for one of the scenes. Rewrite the scene as a radio play and record on tape, complete with music and sound effects.

2. This novel was first published in 1971. Find out what types of music were popular with young people in that year, and listen to the lyrics. What concerns were being expressed? Compare the lyrics of some popular 1971 songs with some of your favorites today. Look for similar themes.

Social Studies

The "hippie movement" began in the late 60s as a revolt against "the establishment." What is "the establishment" and what were the hippies protesting? Do you think there is a similar movement today?

Current Events

Have students create a bulletin board display of articles in recent newspapers or magazines that treat topics or situations like those in the story (e.g., an article about drug dealers, an editorial about underage drinking, a news item about racial harassment, etc.). In each case, students should caption the article by explaining the connection with the story.

EVALUATION: RUBRIC FOR ESSAY-WRITING

The following is a suggested set of criteria for grading student essays. It can be altered in any way that fits the specific needs of a class. We encourage you to share the evaluation criteria with your students *before* they write their essays. You may even want to use this form as a self-grading or partner-grading exercise.

<u>Criterion</u>	<u>Maximum # Points</u>
1. <u>Focus</u>: Student writes a clear thesis and includes it in the opening paragraph.	10
2. <u>Organization</u>: The final draft reflects the assigned outline; transition words are used to link ideas.	15
3. <u>Support</u>: Sufficient details are cited to support the thesis; extraneous details are omitted.	15
4. <u>Detail</u>: Each quote or reference is explained (as if the teacher had not read the book); ideas are not redundant.	15
5. <u>Mechanics</u>: Spelling, capitalization, usage are correct.	15
6. <u>Sentence structure</u>: The student avoids run-ons and fragments. There is an interesting variety of sentences.	10
7. <u>Verbs</u>: All verbs are in the correct tense; sections in which plot is summarized are in the present tense.	10
8. <u>Total effect of the essay</u>: clarity, coherence, overall effectiveness.	10

TOTAL: _____

Comments: